Fact

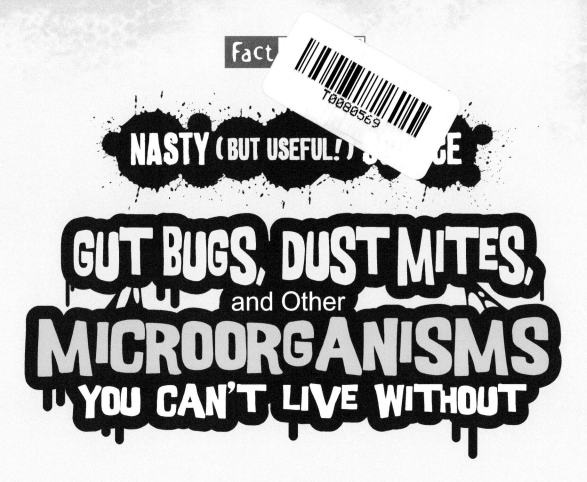

NASTY (BUT USEFUL!) SCIENCE

GUT BUGS, DUST MITES, and Other MICROORGANISMS YOU CAN'T LIVE WITHOUT

by Mark Weakland

Consultant:
Brent Berwin, PhD
Professor, Microbiology and
Immunology Department
Dartmouth College
Lebanon, New Hampshire

CAPSTONE PRESS
a capstone imprint

Fact Finders are published by Capstone Press,
1710 Roe Crest Drive, North Mankato, Minnesota 56003.
www.capstonepub.com

Library of Congress Cataloging-in-Publication Data
Weakland, Mark.
 Gut bugs, dust mites, and other microorganisms you can't live without / by Mark Weakland.
 p. cm.—(Fact finders. Nasty (but useful!) science)
 Summary: "Describes the science behind microorganisms that people couldn't live without,"—
Provided by publisher.
 Includes bibliographical references and index.
 ISBN 978-1-4296-4538-6 (library binding)
 ISBN 978-1-4296-6346-5 (paperback)
 1. Microorganisms—Miscellanea—Juvenile literature. 2. Bacteria—Miscellanea—Juvenile literature.
I. Title. II. Series.
 QR57.W43 2011
 579—dc22   2009050346

Editorial Credits
Jennifer Besel, editor; Matt Bruning, designer; Eric Manske, production specialist

Photo Credits
Alamy: medicalpicture/Kage, 17 (mite), Phototake/MicroScan, 19 (mold); iStockphoto: Henrik Jonsson,
5 (bacteria), sabrina dei nobili, 21, 29 (curd); Newscom: BSIP, 5 (fungi); Science Source: Andrew Syred,
15, Gerd Guenther, 25, 29 (algae), Scimat, 21 (bacteria), SPL, 9, Steve Gschmeissner, 11 (bacteria);
Shutterstock: Damian Herde, 27 (nematode), Damon Roskilly, 5 (algae), Ivan Cholakov Gostock-dot-
net, cover (bacteria), Julius Elias, 19 (orange), Kateryna Kon (bacteria), 7, 13, 29 (top right, bottom
left), Kheng Guan Toh, 21 (factory), Knorre, 23 (yeast), kzww, 23 (bread), Liv friis-larsen, 13, 29 (feet),
Monkey Business Images, 11 (mouth), Nayashkova Olga, 21 (cheese), photobank.kiev.ua, 17 (bed),
Roman Sigaev, 25, 29 (ocean), Sebastian Kaulitzki, cover (mite), 7, 29 (intestines), VOJTa Herout, 26, zcw,
27 (microscope)

Artistic Effects
iStockphoto: Dusko Jovic, javarman3; Shutterstock: belle23, cajoer, Pokaz

TABLE OF CONTENTS

MIGHTY MICROBES

They flavor Swiss cheese. They eat up dead animals. They make armpits stink. What are they? They're microorganisms!

Microorganisms are tiny, living creatures. Micro means invisible to the eye. An organism is a living thing. Put the words together, and you have microorganism—the world's smallest life form. In most cases, a microorganism consists of just a single **cell**. Although they're small, microorganisms can do big things. They make the oxygen you need to stay alive. They're used in medicines that cure infections. They even keep your skin healthy.

Bacteria, fungi, and algae are just a few kinds of **microbes**. Each of these types do a different job. Some are able to turn light into the energy they need in order to live. Others make the gas that makes bread rise. These little critters are very hard workers.

cell: the smallest unit of a living thing

microbe: another word for microorganism

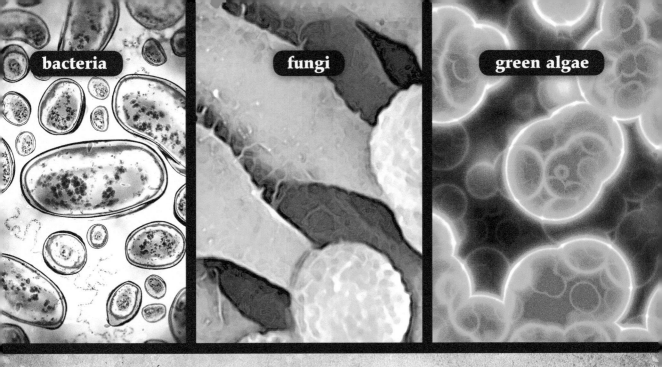

bacteria

fungi

green algae

Microbes live everywhere. Armies of them swirl through your gut. Tough ones live deep in the ocean and high on mountains. Microbes travel too. They float in water and are blown by the wind. They are even carried by food.

In a nutshell, microorganisms are important to life on Earth. Although you can't see them, you can't live without them.

GUT BUGS

Right now, tiny critters are wriggling around inside you. You can't see or feel them. These wriggling microorganisms are bacteria. And your intestines are filled with billions of them.

The bacteria in your small intestine do some important jobs. For starters, they make **nutrients** like vitamins K and B12. Vitamin K makes your blood become thicker, or clot. Without vitamin K, even a small cut would bleed and bleed.

Bacteria in your small intestine also help your body digest food. They do this by breaking **carbohydrates** into usable sugars. The hamburger and fries you munch at lunch have carbohydrates. As the bacteria nibble on your food, the carbs are turned into sugars. Your body uses the sugars to make the energy you need to ride your bike and play video games.

nutrient: a substance needed by a living thing to stay healthy

carbohydrate: a substance found in foods that gives you energy

Between 300 and 1,000 different kinds of bacteria live in your gut. Together they weigh about 3 pounds (1 kilogram).

intestinal bacteria

small intestine

large intestine

Having a gassy day? Blame it on your bacteria! Microbes in your large intestine make your poop and farts stink.

Bacteria in your large intestine break down fiber. Fiber is a carb found in fruits, vegetables, and grains. To break down these foods, bacteria use a chemical process called **fermentation**. During fermentation, fiber is broken down into simple sugars your body can use.

As the bacteria break down food, a lot of fizzy gas is made. That gas has to be released, and it comes out as a fart. Some of this gas contains smelly chemicals like hydrogen sulfide. And that's why your farts raise a real stink when they exit your body.

FOUL FACT

Poop is more than just undigested food. On average, each pound of poop is 60 percent dead microbes.

fermentation: a chemical change that produces fizzy gas

food (yellow) and bacteria (purple) in the intestines, magnified about 400 times

TROUBLEMAKERS

Most microorganisms are helpful to us. Or at least they don't bother us. But there are a few kinds of microbes that our bodies would rather live without. A kind of red algae can cause death if eaten. And bacteria that float in the air can cause pneumonia or tuberculosis. But don't worry! There are more helpful microorganisms in the world than harmful ones.

ZOO IN YOUR MOUTH

Before you brush away your morning breath, stop for a minute. Run your tongue over your teeth. There you'll feel a living layer of slime. It's made up of millions of bacteria and their waste products.

Like other parts of your body, your mouth contains hundreds of different microbes. But that zoo in your mouth is useful. As you chew your toast, bits of food stick to your teeth and tongue. Mouth bacteria munch on those tiny pieces. As they eat, microbes break carbohydrates into sugars and begin the process of food digestion.

As they digest food, bacteria give off some stinky **acids**. These acids cause bad breath. But there are other bacteria that help with that too. Odor-eating bacteria live on your tongue and gums. Scientists think these bacteria get rid of the stinky acids.

acid: a strong liquid that breaks down food

So why do you need to brush your teeth? Without regular brushing, a film of bacteria waste will form on your teeth. It's not sugar that causes cavities. It's bacteria. The more sugar you eat, the more you feed your mouth microbes. And the more sugar the microbes eat, the more acid they produce as waste. This acid waste attaches to your teeth, causing cavities to form. You build a new layer of helpful microbes each day. Brushing helps control the microbe's acid waste.

SMELLY SKIN

Your skin supports about 1 trillion bacteria. They live in your belly button and butt. They wiggle in the creases of your nose. And they crawl in the spaces between your toes.

Having all of these bacteria around is a good thing. The bacteria on your skin keep you healthy. All these good skin bacteria crowd out harmful bacteria that could cause skin infections. They also make a moisturizing substance that keeps your skin soft.

Skin bacteria need warmth for growing and sweat for eating. Your armpits and feet are perfect places for bacteria. As you sweat, your bacteria are having a feast. By itself, sweat is odorless. But as bacteria eat it, the sweat is changed into a stinky chemical. Smells coming from your armpits and feet let you know that your useful skin bacteria are hard at work.

skin bacteria

Unwashed feet often have a "cheesy" smell. The bacteria between your toes produce the same acid given off by the bacteria used to make Swiss cheese!

FACE THE FACTS

Little hairs cover every person's face. Microorganisms called **follicle** mites live in those hairs. Follicle mites are relatives of eight-legged spiders. But they're not short and wide like spiders. Instead, the mites are long and thin, letting them fit snuggly inside a hair follicle. Scales that cover the mite's body help it stay anchored.

Follicle mites are not single-celled creatures. But you still can't see them without a microscope. Follicle mites make their home in skin pores on your face. And there can be a lot of these critters. A family of 25 mites can live in a single follicle.

Although they're creepy, the mites aren't harmful. They quietly munch on the oils that leak out of your pores. They use their tiny claws and sharp mouthparts to feed all the time. While they eat, these guys do their part to crowd out harmful microbes that fly by.

follicle: a hollowed-out space from which hair grows

Follicle mites move around on your skin. They crawl across your face on stubby little legs. The mites are just looking for a new source of food. Once they find a new pore, they'll start feeding again. Follicle mites also find time to lay eggs on your face. It takes just 14 days for a mite to go from egg to adult.

FOUL FACT

When a follicle mite dies, its body turns to liquid. This liquid is then absorbed into your skin.

follicle mite magnified about 800 times

BUGS IN BED

Millions of microbes live on and in your body. But millions more live all around you. In fact, you share your bed with up to 2 million microbes. And none of them are wearing pajamas!

Dust mites are tiny eight-legged creatures. They eat skin cells shed by humans and animals. Who needs frosted flakes when you can eat skin flakes for breakfast?

Dust mites live on your mattress, carpet, or other places where shed skin is likely to be found. There's no shortage of food for these hungry guys. Your body sheds almost 1.5 million flakes of dead skin an hour! Dust mites eat the dead skin. If dust mites weren't hard at work, you'd have dust drifts deep enough for sledding.

dust mites

MEDICINAL MICROBES

Microbes have a special place in the medicine cabinet. Fungi and bacteria are used to make medicines that fight infections.

Drugs called antibiotics are made from microorganisms. One famous antibiotic is penicillin. Penicillin is made from microscopic fungi called mold. Look at a wrinkled rotting orange, and you'll see lots of gray-green fuzz. The fuzz is penicillin mold.

In 1928, a scientist named Alexander Fleming accidently discovered the penicillin. He noticed that mold in a dish was killing the bacteria around it. Several years later, scientists were able to use that information to make medicine from the mold. Today patients are given penicillin to cure ear infections, pneumonia, and other illnesses. Microorganisms may have saved your life!

Antibiotics sometimes kill the good microbes in your intestines as well as the harmful ones. Without the right digestive microbes, you can get diarrhea.

mold magnified about 750 times

CREATURES IN THE KITCHEN

Microbes are used to make a wide variety of foods. If it wasn't for bacteria and fungi, you'd never munch a bagel or a slice of pizza. There'd be no gummy worms without algae.

Cheese couldn't be made without microbes either. To make cheese, milk must first be thickened. A microbe called lactic acid bacteria (LAB) is added to milk. LAB ferments the lactose in milk, forming clumps called curds. Cheese-makers press the microbe-filled curds into molds to make blocks. After it's formed, the LAB keep the cheese from spoiling and give it flavor.

FOUL FACT

Yogurt contains the same bacteria that digest food in your intestines. Eating yogurt puts helpful bacteria into your body.

FROM MICROBE TO CHEESE

1 Lactic acid bacteria is added to milk.

3 Curds are pressed into blocks. Bacteria give the cheese its yummy taste.

2 Bacteria cause curds to form in the milk.

Algae microbes are responsible for all the gooey, chewy foods you love. To make foods thick and chewy, food makers add **carrageenan**. This substance is found in the cell walls of algae.

The process of getting carrageenan from algae cells begins with slimy strands of seaweed. Seaweed is really a bunch of algae microbes all clumped together. In a manufacturing plant, seaweed is washed and mixed with a hot chemical solution. The solution breaks the carrageenan away from the cell walls inside the algae. Then the seaweed is rinsed, dried, and chopped.

When added to foods, the carrageenan in the chopped seaweed makes a gel. The gel makes candy bars, ice cream, and gummy worms thick or gooey. Those are some tasty microbes!

carrageenan: a substance in seaweed that is used to thicken foods

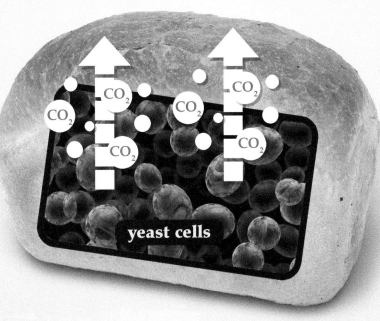

yeast cells

YEAST BEAST

Yeast is a single-celled microbe that makes foods like cinnamon rolls, soft pretzels, and even plain bread possible.

When dried yeast cells are added to warm water, they come alive and begin eating sugar. As the yeast cells eat, they produce carbon dioxide gas (CO_2).

In bread dough, yeast eats the sugars in flour. The carbon dioxide produced by the yeast can't escape the stretchy dough. With the gas trapped inside, the dough puffs up. If it weren't for yeast, a loaf of bread would be as hard as a brick.

HEROES OF THE WORLD

Microorganisms help our bodies stay healthy, and they make the foods we eat. But they do much more than those things. They help our planet too.

Single cells of algae perform **photosynthesis** to make the energy they need to survive. During photosynthesis, algae give off oxygen as waste.

But oxygen isn't waste to people or to the millions of other living things on the planet. We need oxygen to live. Marine algae produce 70 to 80 percent of all oxygen found in Earth's atmosphere. Without oxygen, you, the birds, and the bees would be dead in minutes. Take a deep breath, and thank those microorganisms!

photosynthesis: the process that allows plant cells to use energy from the sun to make food for growth

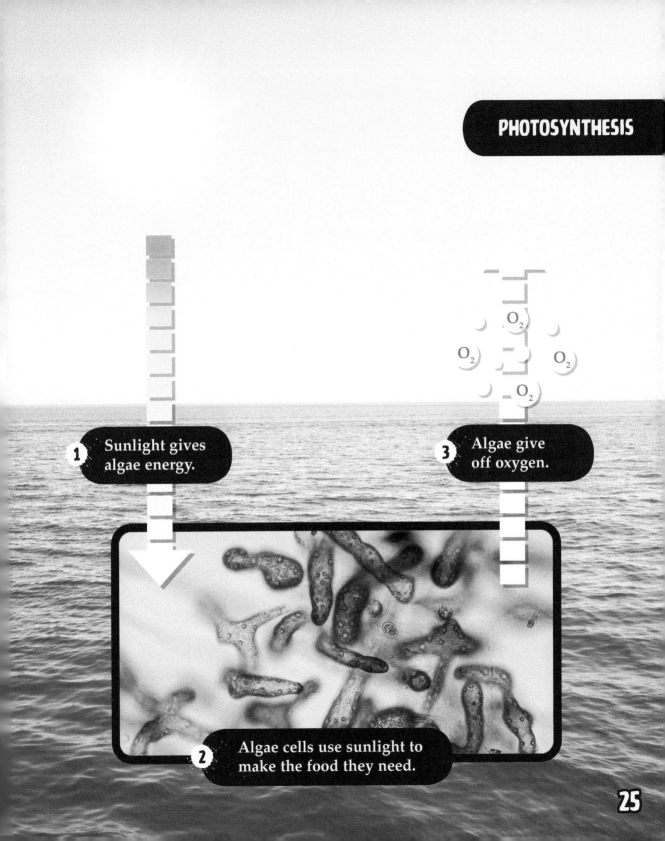

O_2 O_2 O_2 O_2 O_2

1 Sunlight gives algae energy.

3 Algae give off oxygen.

2 Algae cells use sunlight to make the food they need.

Microbes also help the planet by **decomposing** dead things. You'll find bacteria eating up rotting animals and piles of stinking poop. Fungi get nutrients from rotting wood, piles of leaves, and spoiled food.

All this decomposing is important work. If microorganisms didn't do it, we'd be up to our ears in dead stuff. Animal bodies would litter the streets. Mountains of poop would tower in farmyards. By decomposing dead plants and animals, microorganisms get rid of rotting things and put nutrients into the soil.

Fungi help fallen trees decompose.

nematodes

A handful of soil contains thousands of microscopic worms called nematodes. These worms are simple creatures with big appetites. They kill insect pests like wood borers, weevils, and mole crickets.

Nematodes lurk in the soil. Once they find an insect target, the nematodes crawl inside the insect. Inside, they feed on the insect's body. When the insect's body rots, the nematodes spill out and crawl back into the soil.

decompose: to feed on and break down dead matter

THE POWER OF MICROORGANISMS

It's pretty amazing that creatures we can't see make our lives on Earth possible. Microbes make oxygen for us to breathe. They break down food in our bodies. They even keep our skin healthy. And when used by bakers and scientists, microbes help create soft bread, tasty cheese, and healing medicines.

Scientists are studying new ways microbes can help people. Right now, they're using bacteria to produce oil. Algae may one day provide food and oxygen for astronauts traveling to Mars.

No matter where you live or what you do, microorganisms play a huge role in your life. So breathe in some oxygen, and eat a slice of pizza. We can't see them, but microorganisms are there, helping us every day.

GLOSSARY

acid (A-suhd)—a strong liquid that breaks down food

carbohydrate (kar-boh-HYE-drate)—a substance found in foods such as bread, rice, and cereal that gives you energy

carrageenan (kar-uh-GEE-nuhn)—a substance in seaweed that is used to thicken foods and other products

cell (SEL)—the smallest unit of a living thing

decompose (dee-kuhm-POHZ)—to feed on and break down dead matter

fermentation (fur-men-TEY-shuhn)—a chemical change that produces fizzy gas

follicle (FOL-i-kuhl)—a hollow space with a narrow opening from which hair grows

microbe (MYE-krobe)—a living thing that is too small to see without a microscope; microbe is another word for microorganism

nutrient (NOO-tree-uhnt)—a substance needed by a living thing to stay healthy

photosynthesis (foh-toh-SIN-thuh-sis)—the process by which plant cells use energy from the sun to combine carbon dioxide, water, and minerals to make food for plant growth; photosynthesis releases oxygen into the atmosphere

READ MORE

Crewe, Sabrina. *In the Home*. New York: Chelsea Clubhouse, 2010.

Graham, Ian. *Microscopic Scary Creatures*. New York: Franklin Watts, 2010.

Hyde, Natalie. *Micro Life in Soil*. Everybody Digs Soil. New York: Crabtree Publishing, 2010.

Latta, Sara L. *The Good, the Bad, the Slimy: The Secret Life of Microbes*. Prime. Berkeley Heights, N.J.: Enslow Publishers, 2006.

INTERNET SITES

FactHound offers a safe, fun way to find Internet sites related to this book. All of the sites on FactHound have been researched by our staff.

Here's all you do:

Visit *www.facthound.com*

FactHound will fetch the best sites for you!

INDEX